GW00870784

TH

Written by Brian Jones
Illustrated by Andrew Locke

HENDERSON
PUBLISHING PLC

THE EARTH'S SHAPE

A BALL IN SPACE

The Earth is like a huge ball in space. It is spinning around its axis. This is an imaginary line passing through the Earth's centre. The ends of the axis are located at opposite ends of the planet at points we call the north and south **poles**. Halfway between the poles is an imaginary line running right round the Earth. This is the **equator**. The equator divides the Earth into two halves which we call **hemispheres**. There is a northern hemisphere and a southern hemisphere.

DID YOU KNOW?

The Earth is not a true sphere. It is actually flattened at the poles. The Earth measures 42 kilometres more across the equator than it does through the poles.

EARTH FACTS

- Diameter (across equator):
  12,756 km

- Diameter (across poles):
  12,714 km

- Distance around equator:
  40,074 km

- Distance around poles:
  39,942 km

- Weight:
  5,976,000,000,000,000,
  000,000 tonnes

- Volume:
  1,080,000,000,000 cubic km

THE EARTH IN SPACE

THE EARTH AND MOON

The Earth is not on its own in space. Our planet has a Moon orbiting it. The Moon is a quarter of the size of the Earth.

MOON FACTS
- Diameter:
  3,476 kilometres
- Distance around equator:
  10,920 kilometres
- Distance from Earth: 384,365 kilometres
- Time taken to orbit the Earth: 27.32 days

THE SOLAR SYSTEM

The Earth is one of nine planets revolving around the Sun and is the third planet out from the Sun. The Sun's gravity stops the planets from speeding away into space. The Earth is 149,600,000 kilometres from the Sun and orbits the Sun at a speed of 30 kilometres per second. It takes 365 days to complete one orbit. We call this a year.

DID YOU KNOW?

A year is the time taken for a planet to go round the Sun. Mercury is the closest planet to the Sun. It takes just 88 days to complete one orbit. Pluto is the furthest planet. A year on Pluto is equal to 248 Earth years!

THE GALAXY

The Solar System is just a tiny part of a huge galaxy. We call this galaxy the Milky Way. The Milky Way contains 100,000 million stars! The Milky Way is shaped rather like a huge Catherine wheel in space. There are millions of other galaxies in the Universe. Some of these are much bigger than our own.

LARGEST PLANET

The largest planet in the Solar System is Jupiter. Jupiter is so large that, if it were hollowed out, over 1,000 Earths could fit inside!

ECLIPSE OF THE SUN

The Moon is a lot smaller than the Sun. It is also a lot closer. When we look at the Sun and Moon in the sky they both look to be the same size. Sometimes the Moon can pass between the Sun and Earth. When this happens the Sun's light is blocked off. We call this a solar eclipse. When an eclipse happens the sky can go quite dark for a short time.

ECLIPSES OF THE MOON

The only reason that we see the Moon is because it is lit up by sunlight. The Earth casts a shadow into space. If the Moon goes into the Earth's shadow the sunlight is blocked off. The Moon then appears quite dim for a while. We call this a lunar eclipse.

HOW THE EARTH FORMED

A PLANET IS BORN

Astronomers think that the Earth and planets formed about 4,600,000,000 years ago. The Solar System was once a huge spinning cloud of gas and dust. The gas and dust at the centre of the cloud collected together to form the Sun. The rest of the cloud formed a disc round the Sun which split up to form the planets.

NOT TOO HOT, NOT TOO COLD!

We get nearly all our light and heat from the Sun. Without the Sun there would be no life on Earth. Our planet would be a dark, lifeless ball of rock. There would be no water. No plants could grow and animals (including humans) could not survive.

LIFE ELSEWHERE?

There are billions of stars in the Universe and some astronomers believe that there may be planets orbiting them. Some of these planets may have life on them and we may not be alone in the Universe.

DID YOU KNOW?

Luckily, we are at just the right distance from the Sun. If we were any closer the Earth would be too hot for life to survive. If it were further away, our planet would be too cold.

INSIDE THE EARTH

THE EARTH'S OUTER SKIN

When the Earth formed it was molten. As our planet cooled after it formed, all the lightest substances inside the Earth floated up to the surface. These cooled down to form a thin outer layer we call the crust. The Earth's crust is split up into a number of plates and is a bit like a huge jigsaw. These plates slowly move around the surface of our planet.

MANTLE

The mantle is a layer of hot rock around 2,900 km deep which lies beneath the crust. Some parts of the mantle are soft and runny. The different plates forming the crust float on top of the mantle.

THE EARTH'S CORE

The Earth has both an outer core and an inner core. The outer core is 2,200 km thick and is made up of molten metal. It contains mainly iron and nickel. The inner core is the hottest part of the Earth with a temperature of 3,700°C. It is a solid metal ball measuring 2,500 km across.

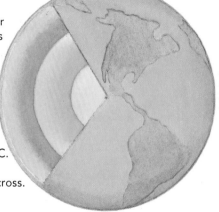

UNDER PRESSURE!

The pressure of the material making up the rest of our planet pressing down on the Earth's core is equal to 3,800 tonnes per square cm. This is well over 3 million times the atmospheric pressure at the Earth's surface!

ROCKS

ROCKS IN THE CRUST

The Earth's crust contains three main types of rock. These are igneous rocks, sedimentary rocks and metamorphic rocks. Each of these was formed in a certain way.

IGNEOUS ROCKS

Igneous rocks are rocks formed from lava which has cooled down and solidified. Some igneous rocks, like granite, solidified underground and some, such as obsidian, solidified on the surface. Obsidian is black and glassy in appearance. It was used by early Mexican tribes for making tools and sculptures.

SEDIMENTARY ROCKS

Sedimentary rocks were formed from particles which formed hard layers underground. These rocks cover more than two-thirds of the Earth's surface. Coal is a sedimentary rock. This was made from deposits of vegetation which became buried over millions of years. Eventually the pressure of the Earth's crust pushing down on it turned the particles into coal. There is a great deal of coal in the Earth's crust. Mankind has been mining coal for hundreds of years to burn for heat and energy.

METAMORPHIC ROCKS

Metamorphic rocks are rocks of the other two sorts which were changed, either by pressure or by heat. Marble is a metamorphic rock which was made from sandstone altered by heat. Slate is another metamorphic rock. This was formed from a mixture of silt and clay called shale. The shale was hardened by heat and pressure to form slate. Slate was used quite a lot for roofing buildings although it is difficult to mine. It isn't used as much now except for re-roofing old and historic buildings.

CONTINENTAL DRIFT

PANGAEA

Because the Earth's crust is always moving, the Earth has not always looked the same as it does today. At one time, about 200 million years ago, all the Earth's land masses are thought to have been joined up in one huge continent. Scientists call this continent Pangaea.

LET'S SPLIT!

Around 135 million years ago the continent of Pangaea split into two parts. The northern part, known as Laurasia, itself split up to form North America, Europe and Asia. The southern part, Gondwanaland, went to form Antarctica, Africa, India, Australia and South America. The continents we see today may have started actually taking shape about 65 million years ago.

INTO THE FUTURE

The continents are still moving around and the Earth's surface may change a lot more. It is thought that Eurasia and Alaska may eventually be joined together. It may be that North and South America and Australia may collide with Asia, therefore forming another huge continent. Africa and Europe would be left together as would Antarctica.

COASTLINES

GOLDEN SANDS

When we think of coastlines
we think of sandy beaches.
Sand is actually rock which
has been worn down by the
weather and by the constant
battering of the sea. There
are lots of different colours
of sand. White sand contains
coral and seashells. Yellow
sand contains tiny pieces of
quartz. Black sand contains
lava while minute fragments
of the gem garnet are found
mixed in with red sand.

DID YOU KNOW?

If you could put all the Earth's coastlines together they
would stretch a distance of just over 500,000km.

CHANGING COASTLINES

The Earth's coastlines are constantly changing. As waves come to shore they can eat into the base of cliffs. Over long periods of time parts of the cliff can tumble into the sea. Very old maps often show villages and buildings near the coast which are not there any more. This is because the sea has worn away the land that they stood on. In 1993 a hotel in Scarborough, Yorkshire, England, collapsed into the sea after the coastline had been eroded away.

LIFE ON THE SEASHORE

ROCK POOLS

The seashore is teeming with life. We have all seen seaweed scattered across the beach when the tide has gone out. Rock pools appear as sea water is left behind when the sea has gone. The pools may contain lots of creatures including crabs, fishes and mussels.

SHELLS

Shells are also found dotted all over the beach. These are home to lots of different creatures. The most common are scallops, limpets, winkles, whelks and mussels. Molluscs live in the unusually-shaped razor shells which are often seen sticking out of the sand. Usually we find shells empty. This is because seabirds have fed upon the creatures as they were left behind during low tide.

SEAWEEDS

Seaweed is the common name given to the huge number of plants found growing from the high water level to depths of between 100 and 200 metres. They are found in many colours including green, red and brown. Many have special air bladders to help keep them afloat in the water. Many types of seaweed can be eaten and some species are even farmed.

DID YOU KNOW?

Hermit crabs have soft bodies and live in empty shells of whelks and winkles to protect themselves. As they grow, they find bigger shells to live in.

LARGE LAND MASSES

A continent is one of the Earth's large land masses.
There are seven continents. These are Africa, Antarctica,
Asia, Australia, Europe, North America and South America.
The continents are really huge sections of the Earth's crust.
These sections are called CONTINENTAL PLATES.
These plates float around the Earth's surface.

THE CONTINENTS

CONTINENT	AREA (Sq km)
Asia	44,000,000
Africa	30,097,000
North America	24,000,000
South America	17,854,000
Antarctica	13,727,000
Europe	10,400,000
Australia	7,682,000

DID YOU KNOW?

The most densely populated continent is Asia. A total of 2,778,000,000 live on the Asian continent. The least densely populated continent is Antarctica. The population of Antarctica is made up of the small number of scientists who are based at scientific research stations.

SUPERCONTINENTS

When two continents drift together a supercontinent is
formed. The boundary between the two continents is
marked by a mountain range. This forms as the crust is
forced upwards as the two land masses are pushed together.
Europe and Asia together form a supercontinent. The Ural
Mountains were formed as Europe and Asia came together
300 million years ago.

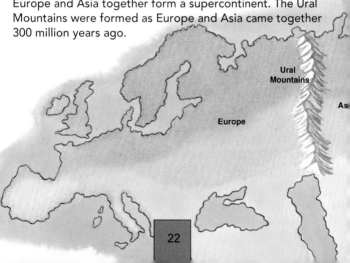

Ural
Mountains

Europe

As

MOVING APART

Sometimes a continent may
split in two. This is
happening now in Africa.
Eastern Africa is breaking
away from the main African
land mass. The Great Rift
Valley in Eastern Africa is the result.
As the two land masses move apart,
the land between them is slumping
down. The result is a huge valley
stretching across the African continent.

Africa

**The
Great
Rift
Valley**

SMALLER BITS

India and Antarctica split away from the main African
continent around 200 million years ago. India collided with
Asia and the Himalayan mountain range was formed. As India
broke away from Africa, pieces of the continent broke away.
These can be seen today as islands in the Indian Ocean.

WHERE LAND MEETS SEA

CONTINENTAL SHELF

A continental shelf is a gently-sloping ledge that lies below the sea. Each continent is surrounded by a continental shelf. The water above the continental shelf is less than 200 metres deep. The true boundaries of the continents are at the edges of the continental shelves.

SHELF WIDTH

The average width of the continental shelf is about 75 kilometres, although this varies quite a lot. The shelf on the Pacific coast of South America is only 1 km wide. However, the shelf around northern Siberia is over 1,000 kilometres wide.

CONTINENTAL SLOPE

Beyond the edge of the shelves the ocean floor descends more steeply. This is the continental slope. Beyond this is the continental rise which drops down to the deep, flat plain of the ocean floor.

DID YOU KNOW?
Most of the food we get from the sea is found in the waters lying above the continental shelf.

WHAT IS AN ISLAND?

An island is an area of land surrounded by water. There are different types of island. Volcanic islands are formed as volcanoes erupt on the sea floor. Molten rock builds up until it breaks through the sea surface. A line of weaknesses in the ocean floor may produce a string of volcanic islands. Continental islands form when a block of land near the shore slips down because of a fault in the Earth's crust. This leaves the highest areas sticking out above the sea.

WORLD'S LARGEST VOLCANOES

A pair of huge volcanoes make up the island of Hawaii. These are Mauna Kea (the world's largest island volcano) and Mauna Loa (the world's largest active volcano).

THE LARGEST ISLAND

The largest island in the world is Greenland. Its area is 2,175,600 square kilometres. The people of Greenland live around the coast. This is because the whole of the interior of Greenland is covered by a vast ice sheet.

THE LARGEST ISLANDS

ISLAND	LOCATION	AREA (sq kms)
Greenland	Between North Atlantic and Arctic Oceans	2,175,600
New Guinea	Southwest Pacific	775,213
Borneo	West Pacific	754,000
Madagascar	Indian Ocean	587,041
Baffin	Canadian Arctic	507,450
Sumatra	Indonesia	473,600

GROUPS OF ISLANDS

There are many groups of islands. The largest is Indonesia which has 13,677 islands with a total area of 1,919,443 sq km. Indonesia lies north-west of Australia between the Pacific and Indian Oceans.

The Aleutian Islands is a chain of volcanic islands in the North Pacific Ocean. It forms part of Alaska and stretches over 1,900 km. There are over 100 islands, all of which are mountainous, barren and treeless.

UNIQUE WILDLIFE

Many islands contain unusual animals. Sometimes these animals are found nowhere else in the world. This is because they are isolated on the islands where they live and don't come into contact with other animals. The Galapagos Islands in the Pacific Ocean are home to many unusual animals including giant tortoises, which can live for up to 200 years, and land iguanas. These are large lizards unique to the Galapagos Islands, which can grow up to 1.2 metres long.

EARTHQUAKES

Earthquakes are caused by movements in the Earth's crust. Most take place along fault lines where the edges of the plates making up the Earth's crust rub against each other. Any movement in the Earth's crust is an earthquake. Most earthquakes last less than a minute. Some do last longer. An earthquake in Alaska in 1964 lasted seven minutes and one in Portugal in 1755 lasted 10 minutes.

DETECTING EARTHQUAKES

Movements in the Earth's crust are detected by a special instrument called a seismograph. These are very sensitive and will detect movements that would not otherwise be noticed.

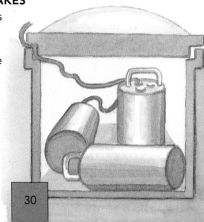

MEASURING EARTHQUAKES

The power of an earthquake is measured on the Richter Scale. Tiny movements in the Earth's crust may measure only 1 on the Richter Scale. Each number on the scale is ten times more powerful than the number below. The most powerful earthquake recorded so far was in 1906 off the coast of Columbia. This measured 8.9 on the Richter Scale.

WORST EARTHQUAKE

The most devastating earthquake ever took place in 1556 in the Shanxi Province of China (now known as Shansi). It is thought that 830,000 people were killed.

LANDSLIDES

SLIPPING AWAY!

A landslide is a downward movement of soil and rock. These happen on hillsides and slopes. If an underground layer of clay becomes wet it might not be able to hold the soil and rock above it. This then slides along the clay and down the slope.

HOLDING TOGETHER

Normally the soil on a hillside or mountainside is held together by the roots of plants and trees growing in it. If these are taken away, landslides can take place. This has happened when hillsides have been cleared to plant crops.

SLOWLY DOES IT

Sometimes the surface soil only moves very slowly. This is called soil creep. It may only move a centimetre or so a year. It can only be seen by the effect it has on things growing in the soil or placed in the ground. Telegraph poles may start to lean over and walls and fences may start to tilt to one side.

VOLCANOES

HOT VENTS

A volcano is a vent in the Earth's crust. Volcanoes are usually shaped rather like a huge cone with a hole in the top called a crater. Molten rock, lava, ash and gas is thrown out of volcanoes through the crater. Many volcanoes are found where the Earth's land masses meet. Here material finds its way through the Earth's crust to the surface. There are about 600 active volcanoes on the Earth. Nearly 100 of these lie on the ocean floor.

DID YOU KNOW?

Volcanoes got their name from the island of Vulcano which lies just to the north of Sicily in the Mediterranean Sea. Long ago the people who lived there thought that Vulcano was the chimney of the forge of Vulcan, the blacksmith of the Roman gods.

CALDERA OR CRATER?

Many volcanoes have a crater at their peak. However, these craters can sometimes collapse into hollows near the top of the volcanoes. Craters that have collapsed like this are called calderas.

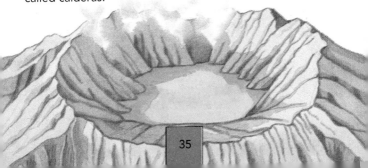

WITH A BANG OR A WHIMPER!

When volcanoes erupt they can throw
out material with explosive force.
These volcanoes, such as Mount
Vesuvius in Italy, can send hot
rocks and lava high into the air.
Many other volcanoes are
much quieter. The material
they eject rises out of the
crater and flows over
the crater rim and down
the sides of the volcano.

HOT RIVERS

The lava that flows from volcanoes is very hot with
temperatures of over 1,000°C. The speed at which lava
flows down the volcano depends on how thick it is. Some
flows are quite slow, giving people time to get out of the
way. However, when Mount Tolbachik in the USSR erupted
in 1975, the lava flowed at over 150 metres per second!

ACTIVE OR NON-ACTIVE

Not all volcanoes are active. Volcanoes that are thought will not erupt again are classed as being extinct. Volcanoes can go for a long time without erupting and some of these have been thought to be extinct. Mount Pinatubo in the Philippines erupted in 1981 after lying dormant for over 600 years! Another volcano that surprised us was Mount St Helens in Washington State, USA. Mount St Helens erupted in 1980 after being quiet since 1857. The eruption devastated an area of over 600 sq kilometres.

LOUDEST BANG

In 1883 the Indonesian island of Krakatoa erupted violently and with such force that huge tidal waves were created. These tidal waves drowned over 36,000 people on the islands of Java and Sumatra. The explosion that took place when Krakatoa erupted is thought to have been the loudest ever heard. The bang was heard in Australia, nearly 5,000 kilometres away!

LARGEST VOLCANO

The largest volcano known is found on the planet Mars. Olympus Mons measures over 600 kilometres across at its base and towers 25 kilometres above the Martian surface. Its caldera has a diameter of 80 kilometres.

DANGEROUS

It isn't only lava that can cause damage when a volcano erupts. Some eruptions throw huge amounts of ash high into the air which can cover the surrounding area. Others can start huge avalanches of mud or ice and snow.

In 1985 a volcano in Columbia erupted. The avalanche of mud which followed killed 20,000 people as it destroyed the nearby town of Armero.

THE OCEANS

WATER, WATER EVERYWHERE!

An ocean is a great area of salt water. Nearly three-quarters of the Earth's surface is covered by oceans. The total area of water is around 360,000,000 sq km. All the oceans are connected to each other and form one continuous area of water. The total volume of water in the oceans is about 1,300,000,000 cubic kilometres.

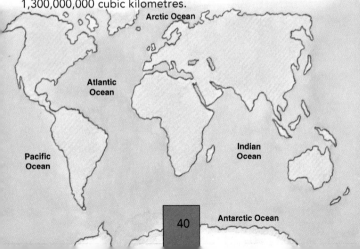

Arctic Ocean

Atlantic Ocean

Pacific Ocean

Indian Ocean

Antarctic Ocean

ONLY THREE

There are really only three oceans - the Pacific, Atlantic and Indian. The Arctic Ocean isn't really an ocean at all, although it is usually regarded as one. The area of sea near Antarctica is often known either as the Antarctic Ocean or the Southern Ocean. However, this ocean is not thought of as a true ocean by geographers.

THE OCEANS

NAME	AREA (sq kms)	AVERAGE DEPTH (metres)	GREATEST DEPTH (metres)
Pacific Ocean	166,242,500	4,188	11,034
Atlantic Ocean	82,217,000	3,330	8,650
Indian Ocean	73,500,000	3,872	7,725
Arctic Ocean	14,350,000	990	4,600

SALTY WATER

The amount of salt in sea water varies, although it is about three percent on average. The saltiest region of the main oceans is the North Atlantic Ocean. The least salty area is the Baltic Sea which contains less than 0.2 percent salt. The water forming the Red Sea in the Indian Ocean is over 25 percent salt!

HOW MUCH SALT?

There is enough salt dissolved in the oceans to cover the Earth's land areas with a layer over 150 metres deep!

MINERAL RICH

Apart from salt, there are over 80 different elements dissolved in sea water including fluoride, calcium, magnesium, potassium, aluminium, copper, manganese and even gold and silver!

HOT AND COLD

The average temperature of the water in the oceans is about 4°C. Sea water freezes at minus 2°C. The warmest waters are found in the Persian Gulf where the temperature can reach over 35°C. The coldest region is the Arctic Ocean. Here the temperature of the water seldom creeps over freezing point.

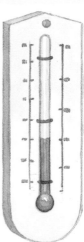

SEAS

A sea is a smaller area of water than an ocean. The world's oceans are split up into different areas. The main area is known by the name of the ocean. The smaller areas are known as seas, bays and gulfs. These are found mainly close to the islands and continents surrounding the oceans.

THE LARGEST SEAS

NAME	AREA (sq kms)	OCEAN
Coral Sea	4,790,000	Pacific
South China Sea	3,680,000	Pacific
Mediterranian Sea	2,966,000	Atlantic
Caribbean Sea	2,750,000	Atlantic
Hudson Bay	1,233,000	Arctic
Baffin Bay	690,000	Arctic
Red Sea	450,000	Indian
Persian Gulf	233,000	Indian

ALL AROUND THE WORLD

The only ocean to stretch right round the world is the Arctic Ocean which completely surrounds the North Pole. The Arctic Ocean is made up of a large number of seas and has a low salt content. This is because a large number of rivers flow into it. These rivers empty huge amounts of fresh water into the Arctic Ocean.

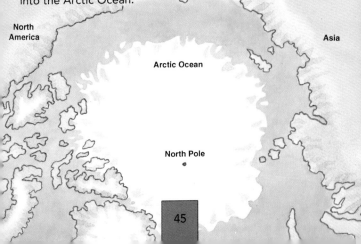

North America

Asia

Arctic Ocean

North Pole

THE OCEAN FLOOR

UNEVEN FLOOR

Nearly half the ocean floor is flat. These areas are called the abyssal plains. They are the flattest places on Earth. However, there are also many mountains and valleys on the ocean floor. Some of the mountains are so tall that they stick out above the surface of the oceans to form islands. There are lots of volcanoes on the ocean floor.

OCEAN DEPTHS

Ocean trenches are the deepest parts of the ocean floor. They are found mainly around the edge of the Pacific Ocean and the northeast Indian Ocean. Ocean trenches are formed where continental plates meet and one of the plates is dragged down below the other.

THE DEEPEST PLACE

The deepest point on the ocean floor is the Mariana Trench in the Pacific Ocean. The bottom of the Mariana Trench lies 11,034 metres below the surface. If you dropped an iron ball into the sea above the Mariana Trench it would take more than an hour to reach the bottom.

OOZE LAYER

Most of the ocean floor is covered by a smooth ooze made up of mud mixed with countless bodies of plants and animals that have drifted down from the surface. It takes thousands of years to build up each centimetre of ooze. The depth of the layer varies. In some places it is around 300 metres deep but at its deepest points the layer is over 10 kilometres thick.

CURRENTS AND WAVES

MOVING WATER

A current is a flow of water in a definite direction. There are three types of ocean current. Drift currents are wide and slow moving. Stream currents are narrow and fast moving. Upwelling currents bring cold water from the bottom of the ocean.

CLIMATE CONTROLLERS

Ocean currents can affect the Earth's climate by carrying warm water from one part of the world to another.

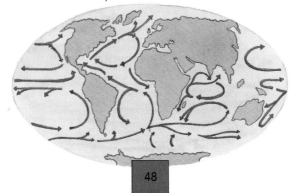

Cold water can also be carried from cold parts of the Earth into warmer regions. The water in currents is kept moving partly by the Earth's rotation and partly by winds moving the water at the ocean surface.

LARGEST CURRENTS

A number of the largest currents are in regions near the equator. These are the equatorial currents. The largest ocean current of all is the West Wind Drift which carries water around the Antarctic. The West Wind Drift carries 2,200 times as much water as the Amazon, the world's mightiest river.

GULF STREAM

The Gulf Stream branches off from the equatorial current and flows northwards from the Gulf of Mexico. It spreads out to form a drift current and brings warm water to the British Isles and Western Europe. Without the warming effect of the Gulf Stream the climate in Britain and parts of Europe would be colder.

BLOWING WATER

Waves are caused by the wind blowing across the surface of the sea. The harder and longer the wind blows, the greater are the waves that are formed. Winds that blow across thousands of kilometres of ocean produce large waves. When they reach shallow water they rear up and become so tall that people are able to surf on them.

GIANT WAVES

Earthquakes and volcanic eruptions beneath the sea can cause giant waves to form. These waves are called tsunamis. When out at sea tsunamis may be only a few metres tall. However, when they reach shallow water they can become very high. The largest ever recorded was seen near Ishigaki Island, Japan in 1971. This was 85 metres high! Tsunamis can move at speeds of up to 800 kilometres per hour and can cause a great deal of damage as they hit the shore and sweep inland.

HIGHEST WAVE

The highest natural wave ever recorded was 34 metres high. This was spotted in 1933 by sailors on board the USS Ramapo.

LIFTING WATERS

Tides are the rising and falling of sea level caused by the Sun and Moon. The gravity of the Sun and Moon pull the water in the oceans into a bulge on either side of the Earth. Tides make the sea level rise and fall twice a day.

HIGHEST AND LOWEST

The highest tides are the spring tides. These happen when the Sun and Moon are in line with each other and are pulling in the same direction on the Earth's oceans. The lowest tides happen when the Sun and Moon are at right angles to each other.

DID YOU KNOW?

Tides don't just affect the oceans. When the Moon passes overhead, the ground rises up just like the oceans. Land masses can be lifted by nearly half a metre!

HIGHEST WATER RISE

Tides cause the water level to rise and fall by different amounts in different places on the Earth. The largest rise takes place in the Bay of Fundy, on the Atlantic coast of Canada. Here the sea level changes rapidly, rising and falling by 18 metres!

Quebec

Gulf of
St. Lawrence

New
Brunswick

Bay of Fundy

Nova Scotia

LIFE IN THE OCEANS

LOTS OF FISH

The world's oceans and rivers contain over 20,000 species of fish. These come in many different shapes and sizes. One of the smallest fish is an 11mm long goby found near the Philippines. Compare this with the whale shark which can reach a length of 18 metres and weigh several tonnes!

DARKER AND COLDER

Most sea creatures live within 200 metres of the surface in the sunlit zone. Here the water is usually clear and warm. Below 200 metres and to a depth of about a kilometre the water is much darker and colder. This is called the twilight zone. The deep sea zone lies below the twilight zone. This zone extends down from the twilight zone to the sea bottom. Here the water is black and very cold.

DEEP SEA LIFE

In spite of the dark and cold, many fish live in the deep sea zone. These include the football-fish. This is a deep-sea angler which has a long thin rod growing from its head. This rod has a luminous bulb on the end. The bulb acts like bait to attract fish for the football-fish to eat. Lots of different deep-sea fish attract their prey in this way.

ECHOLOCATION

Some sea creatures use high-pitched sounds, called ultrasound, to help them find their way around and to locate food. The sounds spread out from the creature in all directions and bounce off nearby objects. The sounds then come back to the creature which then sees how loud they are and how long they took to come back. From this they can work out how far away the objects are, their size and direction. This method of 'seeing' by sound is called echolocation. A number of sea dwellers use this method, including dolphins, sperm whales and porpoises.

ULTRASONIC STING

The sperm whale can give off bursts of ultrasound that are so powerful they can stun their meal of fish or squid before they eat it!

FLYING FISH

The Atlantic flyingfish has enlarged fins which help it to glide through the air above the ocean surface. The fish builds up speed underwater and then rises into the air. The flyingfish can stay out of the water for about 10 seconds, gliding for up to 90 metres in this time!

CORAL REEFS

Coral is a tiny sea creature which lives in the sunlit zone. It has a skeleton made of lime. This is taken out of the surrounding water. Skeletons of coral collect together and build up large formations called reefs. Coral also builds up circular islands called atolls.

An atoll starts out as a coral reef growing on the shores of a volcanic island. If the island sinks it leaves a ring of coral surrounding a circular area of shallow water called a lagoon.

THE GREAT BARRIER REEF

The Great Barrier Reef near Australia is the best known coral formation. It is about 2,000 kilometres long and is made up of coral reefs and islands.

MOUNTAINS

HOW MOUNTAINS ARE FORMED

Most mountain ranges were formed when slabs of the Earth's crust were pushed against each other. If the two slabs buckled up the rocks between them, fold mountains were formed. The Himalayas formed in this way. Sometimes slabs of crust were forced upwards to form block mountains. Volcanic mountains are formed by volcanic action which builds up a pile of molten rock from beneath the Earth's crust.

SOME OF THE WORLD'S HIGHEST MOUNTAINS

MOUNTAIN	LOCATION	MOUNTAIN RANGE	HEIGHT (metres)
Everest	Nepal/Tibet	Himalayas	8,848
K2	Northern India	Karakoram	8,611
Kangchenjunga	Nepal/Sikkim	Himalayas	8,598
Lhotse	China/Nepal	Himalayas	8,516
Makalu	China/Nepal	Himalayas	8,481
Cho Oyu	China/Nepal	Himalayas	8,201

TALLEST MOUNTAIN

The world's tallest mountain is mostly under the sea. This is Mauna Loa in Hawaii. Mauna Loa towers 9,750 metres up from the sea bed. More than half of Mauna Loa lies below the sea.

CLIMBING MOUNTAINS

People who climb mountains are called mountaineers. In 1854 a mountain in Switzerland called Wetterhorn was climbed by Alfred Wills. This started the sport of mountaineering. Mount Everest was first climbed in 1953 by Edmund Hillary and Sherpa Tensing. Nowadays, mountaineering is a very popular sport, although you do need a head for heights!

MOUNTAIN RANGES

LONG RANGES

The longest mountain chain on land is the Andes. Stretching over 7,000 km, the Andes contains many volcanic mountains. It forms the western edge of South America and passes through Colombia, Venezuela, Ecuador, Peru, Bolivia, Chile and Argentina. Second to the Andes is the North American Rocky Mountains. This huge mountain system reaches from Mexico right up through the United States of America and Canada to the border of Alaska, a distance of over 6,000 km.

TALL RANGES

The world's tallest mountain range is the Himalayas which stretches around 3,000 km across Central Asia. The Himalayan range contains nearly 100 of the world's tallest mountains.

LONGEST RANGE

The Earth's longest mountain range runs down the middle of the Atlantic Ocean. The Mid-Atlantic Ridge is 14,000 km long and 1,600 km wide. It stretches almost from the Arctic to the Antarctic. The island of Iceland lies across the Mid-Atlantic Ridge. It was formed by volcanic action from the volcanoes in the Mid-Atlantic Ridge.

MOUNTAIN LIFE

HIGH LIVING!

There are many plants and animals that live high up in the mountains. The higher up you go, the less oxygen there is. Animals (and humans) who live at great heights have developed bigger lungs so that they can take in more oxygen. Some of the highest people in the world are the Kechua Indians. They live nearly 4,000 metres above sea level in the Andes.

GOOD CLIMBERS

Some mountain goats that live in the North American Rocky Mountains are able to climb surfaces that are nearly vertical. This is because they have special pads on their hooves that allow them to grip the slippery surfaces.

GOOD JUMPERS

The higher up a mountain you go, the colder it gets. The snow leopard has long thick fur to keep it warm. The fur is smoky grey with black markings. This is ideal camouflage against the rocky background. The snow leopard, which lives in the Himalayas, is able to make huge jumps across ravines.

HIGH FLYERS

Not many birds are able to live at great heights. The snow partridge can be found feeding and nesting at heights of up to 6,000 metres. Any birds higher than this are only visitors. The Alpine Chough has been seen in mountaineers' camps up to 8,000 metres above sea level!

DEEP GORGES

A canyon is a deep, narrow valley. It runs through mountains. They are also known as gorges. They are formed by streams wearing away the soil and rock. Deeper canyons usually form where there is low rainfall. This is because only the soil and rock under the river bed is worn away. The surrounding land is not worn down by weather erosion.

LONGEST VALLEY

The longest valley in the world is the Great Rift Valley. It stretches around 8,000km across Africa and the Middle East.

GREAT RIFT VALLEY

The Great Rift Valley was formed as two plates in the Earth's crust moved apart. As they did so the land between them slipped down to create the valley we see today. The Great Rift Valley stretches from Mozambique on the African continent to the shores of the Dead Sea in Israel/Jordan.

CHEESY GORGE!

Cheddar Gorge is a narrow, winding gorge cutting through the Mendip Hills in south west England. Its walls tower up to 315 metres above the road that passes through the gorge. Cheddar Gorge is just over 3 km long. Some unusual plants are found in gorges. The Cheddar Pink and Cheddar Hawkweed are only found on the ledges of Cheddar Gorge.

CAVES

CAVE FORMATION

Lots of caves are found in limestone rocks. These are formed by rainwater which dissolves carbon dioxide in the atmosphere as it falls. This makes a weak acid called carbonic acid which then slowly dissolves calcite. This is the main part of limestone rocks. Openings appear in the rock and running rainwater enters these. The rainwater flows through the gaps and holes and wears away the rock to form caverns. Eventually, over thousands of years, the running water forms an underground river system which hollows out systems of caves.

HOLES IN THE GROUND

As rainwater enters the ground it can wear away holes in the rock. These holes are called potholes. They get wider as the water wears away the sides of the pothole. Holes can also be formed if water breaks through the ground and out of the cave system. When this happens a spring is formed.

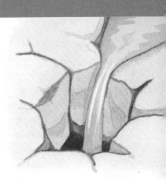

DID YOU KNOW?

• In Kentucky, USA there is a system of caves which has 60,000 potholes leading into it! The cave system itself has a total of nearly 350km of caves and passages.

• One of the largest known caverns in the world is Lobang Nasip Bagus in Sarawak, Malaysia. This huge cavern is 700 metres long and 300 metres wide. The roof of the cavern is at least 70 metres above the floor in all places.

STALACTITES AND STALAGMITES

DRIP, DRIP, DRIP

Water also seeps into caves through the rock from the ground above. The water which has dissolved calcite in it may end up as a drip on the cave roof. It can also drop down onto the cave floor. If the calcite solidifies again it can stay as a tiny lump either on the roof or floor of the cave. More drips appear and the lumps get bigger and bigger. Over time, icicle-like features are formed from the calcite. These can either hang from the roof (stalactites) or reach up from the cave floor (stalagmites).

LONGEST STALACTITE

The longest known stalactite of all is in the Cueva de Nerja, near Malaga in Spain. It is nearly 60 metres long. Part of this huge stalactite is fixed to the wall of the cave which helps to support it.

FREE-HANGING

The longest known free-hanging stalactite is found in a cave in County Clare, Ireland. This is over 11 metres long and hangs down from the cave roof without any other support.

BIG STALAGMITE

The Aven Armand cave in France contains the world's biggest stalagmite, which towers 29 metres above the cave floor.

COLUMNS

If a stalactite and stalagmite join up they can form a column which reaches from floor to roof. The world's largest column is found in Carlsbad Caverns, New Mexico, USA and is over 32 metres high.

CAVE LIFE

HOME SWEET HOME

Thousands of years ago, mankind lived in caves. We have found tools and other items that they used buried on cave floors. Cave people also put paintings on the cave walls and many of these have also been discovered. The best ones are in caves in the Spanish Pyrenees and the French Dordogne Valley.

EXPLORING CAVES

Cavers and potholers carry special equipment with them to help them explore cave systems. They need lights to help them see around and rope ladders to let them climb down steep underground slopes. Some caves are flooded with water. To explore these, special swim suits are needed which help keep the explorers warm in the cold water. They also have oxygen tanks to allow them to breathe as they swim around the underwater cave systems.

CAVE DWELLERS

In spite of caves being dark places, many different animals make their homes there. In Asia, a bird called the cave swiftlet builds its nest from saliva. These nests are glued to cave walls and roofs. Bats are often found in caves, including the Carlsbad Caverns. Here colonies containing millions of bats have been found.

ROCK FORMATIONS

EROSION

The Earth's surface is changing all the time. This is because of something called erosion. Erosion happens when the rocks and soil on the Earth's surface are loosened and worn away. Mountains are being eroded all the time. The ice and frost at the top of the mountain splits and wears away the rock. It is thought that mountains lose nearly a centimetre of rock every hundred years!

STRANGE SHAPES

It isn't only ice and frost that cause erosion. Rivers carve out canyons and valleys and rain can wear away rocks. Underground rivers and streams carve out caves and potholes. There are also many strange rock formations, expecially in desert regions. Sand that is blown through the air rubs against rocks, wearing them away.

RAINBOW BRIDGE

Rainbow Bridge in the Navajo Indian Reservation, Utah, USA is a huge natural arch of rock. It towers to a height of 94 metres and is the highest natural arch in the world. It was formed after the stream we call Bridge Creek wore a hole in a large chunk of rock around 15,000,000 years ago. Once a hole had been formed, the wind and rain gradually widened the hole. While this was going on, Bridge Creek continued to wear away the valley floor. Rainbow Bridge slowly got wider and taller!

THE EARTH'S POLES

THE ARCTIC

The Earth's poles are the cold regions. They lie at the far north and south. The Arctic surrounds the north pole and is really a huge floating mass of ice. It lies in the Arctic Ocean and is almost completely surrounded by land.

COLD AREAS

The Arctic lies within the Arctic Circle and the Antarctic lies inside the Antarctic Circle. In the areas inside the Arctic and Antarctic Circles the winters are long and very cold and the winter night lasts for months. The seas and land remain frozen. In the summer months the ice begins to melt and icebergs break off and drift away.

GREENLAND

Most of Greenland is covered in an ice sheet. This is nearly 2,500 kilometres long and over 1,000 kilometres wide. It is up to 3 kilometres thick in places. The people who live in Greenland can only live near the coast.

ACROSS THE ARCTIC

The American submarine Nautilus was the first to go right across the Arctic Ocean. It passed underneath the Arctic ice in 1958 and travelled right under the north pole.

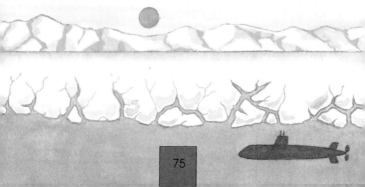

THE ANTARCTIC

The Antarctic surrounds the south pole. The name Antarctic means 'opposite the Arctic'. The Antarctic is land surrounded by ocean. The Antarctic land mass is covered by the largest ice sheet in the world. This has an area of over 12 million square kilometres making it bigger than the United States of America. The Antarctic ice sheet measures 4 kilometres thick in places.

IF THE ICE MELTS...

There is so much water frozen in the Arctic and Antarctic ice sheets that, if it melted, the sea level would rise by more than 50 metres. Lots of cities and towns in coastal areas around the world would be submerged.

EARLY EXPLORERS

The first explorer to sail through the Antarctic Ocean was the Englishman James Cook in 1773-74. Exploration was difficult because his wooden ship could not stand the ice pressure. The first explorer to reach the interior of the Antarctic was the Englishman Robert Scott between 1901 and 1904. The Norwegian explorer Roald Amundsen first reached the south pole in 1911. The American explorer Robert Peary was the first to reach the north pole in 1909.

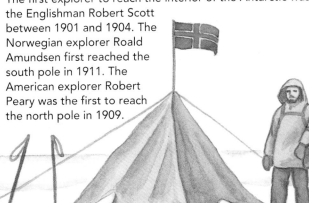

LIFE AT THE POLES

WATER BIRDS

Penguins are flightless birds which have thick feathers to protect them from the cold. The biggest species of penguin is the emperor penguin. They can grow up to 1.2 metres tall. Female emperor penguins lay one egg a year, then swim away! The male penguin keeps the egg warm until it hatches.

BEARING THE COLD

Polar bears are found in the area around the north pole. They can grow up to 2.5 metres long. Polar bears have lots of fur on their feet to help them walk in the snow and thick fur coats to keep them warm. They dig out dens under the ice to live in during the winter months.

STRANGE CREATURES

Some fish in the Antarctic seas have a chemical in their blood to stop them freezing.

The Arctic fox changes the colour of its coat to suit the season - white in winter and browny-red in summer.

DID YOU KNOW?

Scientists have found fossils of apes in Antarctica that look very much like humans. This shows that Antarctica was once much warmer than it is now.

The Antarctic Weddell seal can dive to a depth of 300 metres in search of food.

ICEBERGS

An iceberg is a floating mass of ice. About a tenth of the land on the Earth is covered by ice. Sometimes chunks of ice break away and float off to sea. These chunks are called icebergs. They drift away from the polar regions towards warmer regions until they eventually melt.

Some icebergs have floated so far that thay have been spotted near the equator. One was seen near the island of Bermuda, about 4,000 kilometres from the Arctic!

Icebergs from the Antarctic break away from the Antarctic ice sheet. They are usually flat-topped. Icebergs from the Arctic are much more rugged in shape. About four-fifths of the ice in an iceberg lies below the sea.

Icebergs can be dangerous to shipping. The British liner Titanic struck an iceberg near Newfoundland in 1912. The ship sank and nearly 1,500 passengers were drowned.

LARGEST ICEBERG
The largest iceberg ever seen was spotted in 1956 in the South Pacific Ocean, off the coast of Antarctica. It had come from the Antarctic ice sheet. It measured over 200 miles long and 60 miles wide making it bigger than the country of Belgium!

GLACIERS

A glacier is a huge block of ice which moves slowly across the land. Glaciers are formed from fresh water. About three-quarters of the Earth's total fresh water is frozen inside glaciers.

Most glaciers move very slowly, travelling just a few inches per day. Some travel much faster. Some glaciers in Greenland move at the rate of nearly 30 metres a day. When a glacier reaches a lake or the sea it breaks up to form icebergs.

As a glacier moves it wears away the land and can form valleys and other features. We can see many such features in the landscape today. These were formed during periods of glaciation called ice ages. These happened many times long ago in the Earth's history when the average temperature at the Earth's surface fell. Huge areas of land were covered by ice sheets and glaciers flowed across much of the northern hemisphere.

Some glaciers are really huge. One of the largest known is the Novaya Zemlya Glacier in the USSR. This glacier is over 400 kilometres long.

DID YOU KNOW?
Glaciers cover about a tenth of the Earth's land surface. There is enough ice in glaciers to cover the land to a depth of over 100 metres!

TUNDRA

FROZEN LAND

Tundra are areas of frozen land at high altitudes. They are found between the northern tree line and the Arctic polar region. Tundra lie across northern Canada, Greenland, Scandinavia, northern Asia and part of northern Russia including Siberia. Some tundra is also found in southern South America and the Antarctic.

PERMAFROST

Permafrost happens when a deep layer of soil remains frozen, even during the summer months when the soil above may thaw out. It is thought that about a quarter of the Earth's land surface is permafrost. The layer of permafrost below most tundra is a few hundred metres deep.

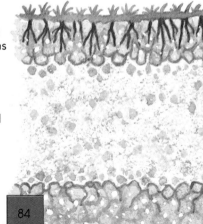

COLDEST PLACE

One of the coldest places on the Earth is Siberia. Here in the tundra the temperature has dropped to as low as minus 70°C! A layer of permafrost over a kilometre deep has been found in Siberia.

ICE HILLS

Underground springs in the tundra can often become frozen. The water may then be forced upwards to form a dome-shaped mound. These small hills of frozen water are called pingos.

TUNDRA LIFE

BOGGY LAND

There isn't a lot of rainfall in the tundra. Because the ground beneath the surface is frozen, what little rain there is can't drain away properly. Shallow areas of water and marshes are found scattered across the tundra. Ducks and geese are found on these areas of water.

LOW-LYING PLANTS

Because of the permafrost, tundra contain very few trees. The vegetation that grows there is mostly grasses, mosses, lichens, heather and sedges. During the winter the ground-hugging plants are covered by a layer of snow.

ANIMALS OF THE TUNDRA

The Arctic fox lives in the tundra, as well as Arctic hares and snowshoe rabbits. During the spring and summer, huge herds of caribou (North American reindeer) wander into the tundra to give birth to their young. Also during the summer, when the temperature creeps above freezing point for a short time, swarms of mosquitoes and other insects invade the tundra.

NEVER ENDING ICE AGE

It is so cold in the tundra that animals which have been extinct for thousands of years have been found deep frozen in the ice!

LAKES AND INLAND SEAS

LAKES

A lake is an area of water located in a low-lying area of ground. They are only connected to the sea by rivers. Most lakes contain fresh water. The water in a lake can come from rivers that feed into it. A lake can also be fed by melting water from a glacier or from rainfall.

THE LARGEST LAKES AND INLAND SEAS

LAKE/INLAND SEA	LOCATION	AREA (Sq km)
Caspian Sea	USSR/Iran	370,990
Lake Superior	USA/Canada	82,071
Lake Victoria	East Africa	69,463
Aral Sea	USSR	64,500
Lake Huron	USA/Canada	59,547
Lake Michigan	USA	57,735
Lake Tanganyika	East Africa	32,880
Lake Baikal	USSR	31,456

DEEPEST LAKE

The deepest lake in the world is Lake Baikal in southeast Siberia, USSR. It is crescent-shaped, 636km long and an average width of 48km. The maximum depth of Lake Baikal is 1,620 metres, just over a mile! More than 300 rivers run into Lake Baikal, although only one, the Angara, drains it. Lake Baikal contains roughly one fifth of the Earth's fresh water.

THE SALTIEST LAKE

The saltiest lake on Earth is the Dead Sea. This lies partly in Israel and partly in Jordan. The Dead Sea contains eight times as much salt as normal sea water. Because there is so much salt, it is almost impossible to sink and the Dead Sea is the easiest place in the world to swim in!

LOWEST PLACE

The shore of the Dead Sea is the lowest point on the Earth's surface. It lies nearly 400 metres below the level of the Mediterranean Sea, which is only 75km away.

LAKE DWELLINGS

Long ago, prehistoric man used to build villages on lakes. They did this by putting supports into the bottom of the lake and building their houses on them. Prehistoric villages have been found in many places including Gt. Britain, Europe, West Africa and South America.

THE HIGHEST LAKE

The highest navigable lake in the world is Lake Titicaca in South America. Located high in the Andes mountains, Lake Titicaca is 177km long and lies between Bolivia and Peru. The surface of Lake Titicaca is 3,800 metres above sea level.

RIVER SYSTEMS

A river is formed from water which flows across the land. The place where a river starts is called its source. The place where it enters the sea or a lake is called its mouth. A river may be joined by smaller rivers. These are called tributaries. The river gets bigger each time a tributary joins it. We call a river and its tributaries a river system.

SOURCES OF RIVERS

Many rivers start as small streams. These may come from melting glaciers or from a lake. A river usually flows steeply downhill near its source. Over millions of years the river may wear a deep channel in the ground over which it flows. As the river nears its mouth the water flows more slowly. This is because the land is less steep.

LARGEST GORGE

A gorge is a valley that has been cut out by a river. The Colorado River flows through the Grand Canyon, the world's largest gorge. The Grand Canyon is 350km long, up to 29km wide and over 1.5km deep in places!

THE WORLD'S LONGEST RIVERS

RIVER	LOCATION	LENGTH (km)
Nile	Northeast Africa	6,695
Amazon	South America	6,570
Chiang Jiang	China	6,300
Mississippi-Missouri	USA	6,020
Ob-Irtysh	USSR	5,600
Huang He	China	5,464

THE MIGHTY AMAZON!

The mighty River Amazon flows from the Andes Mountains across South America and into the Atlantic Ocean. There is so much water in the Amazon that fresh water can be found at the surface 160km out to sea!

Atlantic Ocean

South America

R. Amazon

Andes Mountains

THE LONGEST RIVER

The world's longest river is actually made up of two rivers which join together. The White Nile rises in Lake Victoria which lies across the borders of Kenya, Uganda and Tanzania. The Blue Nile starts from Lake Tana in Ethiopia. They join in Sudan to form the Nile which then flows through Egypt into the Mediterranean Sea.

Mediterranean Sea

Cairo

Egypt

Red Sea

R. Nile

Sudan

Blue Nile

Ethiopia

White Nile

Uganda   Kenya

Lake Victoria

Tanzania

DID YOU KNOW?

The Amazon carries so much water that there are nearly 50,000km of navigable waterways in the Amazon river system!

WATERFALLS

DROPPING RIVERS

A waterfall is a place on a river where water flows over a steep drop. This drop is made as the river wears away the soft rock over which it flows.

FAMOUS WATERFALL

One of the best known waterfalls is Niagara Falls. These lie on the Niagara River which flows between Lake Erie and Lake Ontario, two of the Great Lakes on the Canada-USA border. Niagara Falls is actually two falls - the American Falls and Horseshoe Falls.

MOVING WATERFALLS

Waterfalls slowly wear away the rocks at the edge of the falls. Over thousands of years the waterfall may disappear altogether. This will happen to Niagara Falls which will eventually reach Lake Erie in about 25,000 years from now.

HIGHEST WATERFALL

The world's highest waterfall is Angel Falls in Venezuela. Here the water of the Caroni River drops 979 metres - over three times the height of the Eiffel Tower in Paris, France!

HIGHEST WATERFALLS

WATERFALL	LOCATION	HEIGHT (metres)
Angel Falls	Venezuela	979
Yosemite	California, USA	739
Mardalsfossen South	Norway	655
Tugela	South Africa	614
Cuquenan	Venezuela	610
Sutherland	New Zealand	580

ESTUARIES AND DELTAS

BROAD MOUTHS

Estuaries and deltas are found at river mouths. Estuaries are broad river mouths where tides occur. Both salt water from the sea and fresh water from the river are found here.
A delta is an area of sandbank formed at the mouth of a river. The tides are not strong enough to remove the sand brought down by the river. The river splits up and reaches the sea in a number of mouths.

DID YOU KNOW?

The delta at the mouth of the Nile is shaped like the Greek letter delta (Δ) so giving rise to the name.

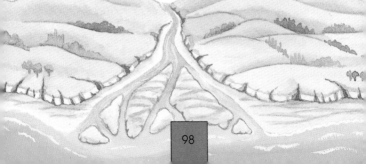

LARGEST DELTA

The largest river delta is the Ganges-Brahmaputra delta. The Ganges rises in Northern India and the Brahmaputra in the Himalayan glaciers. The rivers join up in Bangladesh and flow into the Bay of Bengal. The Ganges-Brahmaputra delta has an area of 75,000 square km. This makes it comparable in size to Ireland!

MIGHTY ESTUARY

The Amazon has an estuary over 100 km wide. Every minute this mighty river pours over 7,000,000 cubic metres of water into the Atlantic. This water passes through a maze of islands and channels which lie in the Amazon estuary.

THE RAIN CYCLE

WATER FROM THE SKY

Rain is water falling in drops from clouds. The water in clouds usually falls to the Earth's surface because it cools. This can happen when the clouds rise above a mountain range. It can also happen if the warm air containing the rain rises over a colder mass of air.

IMPORTANT WATER

Water is very important to life on Earth. It forms a large part of the bodies of humans and other animals. It also provides a home for many forms of wildlife, including fish, birds and insects.

ON THE MOVE

Water is continually being moved between the land, sea and atmosphere. This is called the water cycle, or rain cycle. Water rises into the sky when it is warmed by the Sun's heat. When water rises this way we call it evaporation. The water enters clouds where it condenses to form small droplets. The clouds are blown by winds until they meet colder air. The water then falls to the Earth's surface as rain.

RECYCLING WATER

This can be either back into the sea or onto the land. A lot of the rain that falls onto the land finds its way back to the sea along rivers and streams. Some water ends up in lakes and pools and some ends up being taken in by plants. This then evaporates from the leaves back into the sky, and so helps to keep the rain cycle going.

FORESTS

CONIFEROUS FORESTS

The trees that form coniferous forests have needle-shaped leaves and cones. Typical coniferous trees are the spruce, pine, firs, cypress, redwood and sequoia. Some conifers lose their needles in the autumn, although most conifers are evergreen. Coniferous forests are found in the cold climates of the far north including North America, northern Europe and Asia. They are also found high up in mountains.

TIMBER!

Coniferous forests provide nearly three-quarters of the world's timber. The trees are used to help provide lots of different products including furniture, paper, turpentine, matches and oil for use in soap.

DECIDUOUS FORESTS

The trees forming these forests have broad leaves. They are also deciduous which means that they lose their leaves in autumn. The trees in deciduous forests include oak, beech, elm, ash, birch and maple. Deciduous forests are found in certain areas of Japan and China, New Zealand, western and central Europe and the eastern United States of America.

TALLEST TREE

The Howard Libbey redwood tree is the world's tallest tree with a height of up to 110 metres. These trees can measure over 13 metres around the base! If you think this is wide, one species of sequoia tree measures up to 30 metres around the base. This is wide enough to drive a car through!

TROPICAL RAIN FORESTS

HOT AND WET

Tropical rain forests equal all the other types of forest put together. They grow in areas around the equator where the temperature and rainfall are always high. They can be found in northern Australia, south-east Asia, Central Africa and Central and South America. Less than 10 percent of the Earth's land surface is covered by rainforests, yet they contain over half of all known plant and animal species.

DIFFERENT LAYERS

A rainforest has five layers, each with its own plant and animal life. The top layer of all is the emergent layer. This is made up of the tops of the tallest trees. Birds of prey watch over the forest below from here on the lookout for small animals to catch and eat.

Below this is the canopy. This is made up from the branches and leaves of the tree tops. Here are found most of the forest's animals and plants, including snakes, monkeys and many birds.

The understorey is formed from the tops of smaller trees that do not reach up to the canopy. Part of the understorey includes young trees that will eventually break through into the canopy or understorey.

The shrub layer is made up of shrubs and small trees. If the canopy and understorey are dense, not much sunlight will get through to the shrub layer.

Lowest of all is the herb layer. Made up of undergrowth, the herb layer contains ferns and herbs. Many insects live here, providing food for ground-dwelling animals such as the tapir and the anteater, which comes down from the trees to feed on the many ants which live on the forest floor.

DID YOU KNOW?

The soil on the rain forest floor is only a few centimetres deep. This means that the root systems of the trees are only shallow. The base of the trunks of some large trees spread out over the forest floor to provide them with support.

SAVE THE FORESTS!

Around 50 percent of the world's rainforests have been destroyed. There are many reasons for this. The need for timber is one. Large areas of rainforest are also cut down to provide grazing land for beef cattle. However, the soil in rainforests is only very thin. This is because most of the minerals in the forest are actually contained in the trees and plants themselves. The soil is soon washed away by rain and cattle can no longer graze there. So more rainforest has to be cut down. The destruction goes on and on, and there soon may be no rainforest left.

USE THE FORESTS!

A tropical rainforest can provide lots of things of use to humans, if it is preserved and looked after properly. These include plants for medicine, poisons, different oils, spices and gums, rubber and dyeing materials. There may be other useful products we can get from rainforests, although if we carry on cutting them down we may never find out what they are!

DID YOU KNOW?

It is thought that over 1,500 different rainforest plants could be used as vegetables for us to eat!

WOODLANDS

WOODY AREAS

A woodland is an area where trees grow thickly. Woodlands are not as large as forests. They grow in regions of the Earth between the tropical rainforests and the cold coniferous forests of the north. They need a climate that is mild and moist and grow in regions where there are four distinct seasons. The change in weather over the year helps woodlands to support a varied amount of life.

WOODLAND TREES

Although there are some conifers in woodlands, most of the trees are broad-leaved deciduous trees. These lose their leaves in autumn and grow them again in spring. In woodlands around the Mediterranean Sea and parts of the southern hemisphere most of the trees are evergreen.

ABUNDANT LIFE

A woodland contains a vast amount of life. A typical woodland will contain huge numbers of insects, slugs and worms. These provide food for many birds and mammals. As with rainforests there are a number of different layers to a woodland. The tops of trees support animals and birds which feed on the leaves, flowers and fruit of the trees. Below these, beetles and other insects live on the branches and trunk of the trees. Even fallen trees provide a home for many different types of fungi as well as insects such as woodlice which feed on the decaying wood.

WHAT A CURE!

There are many different species of woodlice. Some of these are able to roll themselves up into a tiny silvery ball if danger threatens. Woodlice are sometimes called pill-bugs. This is because people used to swallow woodlice as a cure for stomach upsets!

WOODLAND PLANTS

There are many plants that live in woodlands. Many flowering plants grow on the ground in the shade of the trees. Some woodland floors are carpeted with flowers such as bluebells or the white wood anemonies. The trees in woodland let sunlight through to the ground. This allows many different plants to grow. Other woodland plants include ferns, mosses and fungi.

LIFE IN LEAF LITTER

Each autumn the trees in woodlands lose their leaves. These fall to the ground and, over the years, build up into a thick carpet which is home to a number of plants. The Horn of Plenty is a black funnel-shaped fungus which grows in the leaf litter of woodlands. Other fungi growing in leaf litter include the bright orange Chanterelle and the aptly named Orange Peel fungus.

GRASSLANDS AND SAVANNAHS

OPEN AREAS

Grasslands are found in areas where there is too little rain to allow forests to grow but where there is enough to prevent deserts forming. They are hot in summer and cold in winter. The Earth's greatest expanses of farmlands are found on grasslands. They can be used for a number of things including growing crops and grazing cattle or other animals.

MAN-MADE GRASSLANDS

All over the Earth man has created grasslands by clearing away woodland and forests to make way for farmland. Where trees once grew, crops are grown and animals graze.

FOOD FROM THE GRASSLANDS

Many grasslands are used to grow crops for feeding humans and animals. These include wheat, rice, rye and barley. Most rice is grown in Asia and is used to feed over half the population of the Earth! Some wheatfields, such as those in North America and Canada, are really huge and cover many square kilometres.

PATCHY GRASS

Savannahs are open tropical grasslands with scattered trees, bushes and shrubs. They cover large areas in regions around the equator. The name was given to treeless plains in South America by Spanish explorers.

DIFFERENT NAMES

Grasslands are found in many places across the Earth's surface including Europe, Asia, North and South America, South Africa and Australia. Each region gives a different name to grasslands. In North America they are known as prairies and in Australia as scrub. South African grasslands are known as veldt and South American grasslands as pampas. The Asian grasslands are called steppes.

DID YOU KNOW?

There are about 9,000 different species of grass distributed across the world. Most of these have long, narrow leaves and hollow stems.

SAVANNAH WILDLIFE

Some of the best known animals live on the African savannah including giraffes, zebras, gazelles and wildebeests. These feed from the vegetation that grows on the savannah. Most of these animals provide food for the big cats such as lions and cheetahs. Many birds of prey stalk the skies scanning the ground for birds, rats and snakes.

SAVANNAH SCAVENGERS

One of the most famous of the savannah birds is the vulture which scavenges from the remains of animals killed by other predators. However, it isn't only the vulture which enjoys other animals' kills. The jackal and hyena, ants and other insects and other birds such as the crow and raven all join in to help devour the animal remains.

DESERTS

DRY AREAS

A desert is an area which has very little rainfall and vegetation. Nearly a third of the Earth's land surface is desert. Not all deserts are sandy. Some are bare rock and some are covered with gravel and pebbles. The icy wastes of the Arctic and Antarctica are actually classed as deserts.

DEATH VALLEY

The hottest and driest place on Earth is Death Valley in southeast California, North America. It got its name from gold prospectors who died there in 1849 because of lack of food and water. Death Valley is 225 kilometres long and between 6 and 26 kilometres wide. It lies 80 metres below sea level and is the lowest place in North America. Temperatures as high as 57°C have been recorded there.

DID YOU KNOW?

Although temperatures in deserts can be extremely high during the day, at night these can drop to below freezing point.

LARGEST DESERT

The world's largest desert is the Sahara in North Africa which has an area of 5,500,000 square kilometres. This is nearly a fifth of the size of Africa itself. The Sahara wasn't always a desert region. At different times in the past it has been under the ocean and has also been covered in forest. Special images from satellites show that there are many dried-up river beds under the surface of the Sahara. This proves that there was running water in the Sahara long ago.

DESERT LIFE

STORING WATER

Plants and animals that live in the desert must be able to store water. This is so they can withstand long periods without rainfall. Cacti store water in their stems. Camels can go without eating and drinking for a long time. This is because they store a food reserve of fatty tissue in their humps. Camels can also withstand large changes of temperature which makes them ideally suited to desert life.

DESERT ANIMALS

There are lots of different animals in deserts. These include snakes and lizards, rodents and birds. Because of the harsh conditions these creatures have had to adapt to life in the desert. The North American jack rabbit has developed long ears which contain lots of blood vessels. This helps it to radiate body heat away.

DESERT PLANTS

Plants have also had to adapt. The skin of a cactus is extremely waterproof to help it keep water in. Some plants, such as the Australian saltbush plant, have developed very long root systems to help them gather what water they can from the soil. Cacti, as well as some bushes and trees, have spikes instead of leaves. This reduces the amount of water that would be lost through the leaves.

NIGHT LIFE

Most desert animals only emerge at sunset or sunrise. This is so that they can avoid the heat of the day. In the Australian desert marsupial mice search for food during the night. They store reserves of fat in their tails in case there is a shortage of food.

DAY AND NIGHT

LIGHT AND DARK

If we look down on the Earth from space we see that only the half of the Earth facing the Sun is actually lit up. It is daytime in this half. The half facing away from the Sun is in the darkness that we call night.

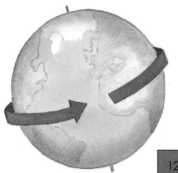

SUNRISE AND SUNSET

The Earth spins once on its axis every 24 hours. It spins from west to east. Because of this, the Sun seems to rise in the east and set in the west.

DAY AND NIGHT

During each 24 hours different places on the Earth's surface are carried first into daylight and then into night. When it is daytime in the United Kingdom, it is night time in Australia. This is because Australia is on the opposite side of the Earth to the United Kingdom.

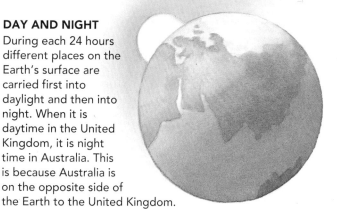

DID YOU KNOW?

The Earth's spin is slowing down by about 1 second every 90,000 years. This might not sound much, but when the Earth was formed long ago our planet took only about 10 hours to spin once on its axis!

THE SEASONS

A TILTED PLANET

The Earth is tilted at an angle in space. As it orbits the Sun first the north pole and then the south pole are tilted towards the Sun. It is the tilt of the Earth that causes the seasons here on Earth.

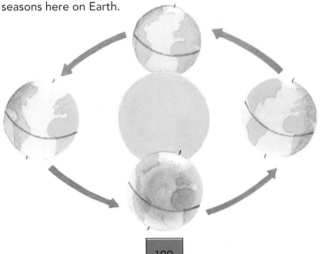

SUMMER AND WINTER

When the northern hemisphere is tilted towards the Sun it is summer in the north. The Sun appears higher in the sky as seen from places north of the equator. It is also in the sky for a longer time so the days are longer and the nights are shorter. When it is summer in the north it is winter in the south. This is because the southern hemisphere is tilted away from the Sun.

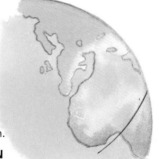

SPRING AND AUTUMN

Around 21st March and 23rd September neither hemisphere is tilted towards the Sun. Day and night are of equal length everywhere. On these dates, spring and autumn start.

LONGEST DAY, SHORTEST NIGHT

Around 21st June each year the northern hemisphere is at its closest to the Sun. It is on this date that the Sun stays in the sky for the longest time and the northern hemisphere has its longest day and shortest night. It is the first day of summer in the north and the first day of winter in the south. At this time the southern hemisphere has its shortest day and longest night.

On or around 21st December the southern hemisphere is at its closest to the Sun. The Sun stays in the sky longer as seen from places south of the equator and it is the longest day and shortest night in the south. It is the first day of summer in the south and the first day of winter in the north. The northern hemisphere then has its shortest day and longest night.

124

DID YOU KNOW?

The actual distance of the Earth from the Sun doesn't cause the seasons. In January, the Earth is at its closest point to the Sun, although it is actually winter in the northern hemisphere.

COLD POLES

The Sun always appears low in the sky as seen from the polar regions. Because of this, the Sun is not able to warm these areas up properly. That is why it is always cold in the Arctic and Antarctic.

LATITUDE AND LONGITUDE

Maps of the Earth show lines running across (from east to west) and up and down (from the north pole to the south pole). The lines running from east to west are lines of LATITUDE.
The equator is actually a line of latitude. The position of any place on the Earth north or south of the equator is called its latitude.
The lines running north to south are lines of LONGITUDE. The main one is the line which runs through Greenwich in London, England.
The longitude of any place on the Earth is its distance from the line of longitude that runs through Greenwich.

THE TROPICS

The Sun can only appear directly overhead from places near the equator. From regions further to the north and south, the Sun's rays always shine down on the Earth at a slant. The Tropic of Cancer and the Tropic of Capricorn are lines of latitude running round the Earth. The Tropic of Cancer is the furthest north that the Sun can appear overhead. This happens during northern summer when the northern hemisphere is tilted towards the Sun.

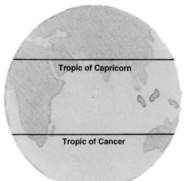

The Tropic of Capricorn is the furthest south that the Sun can appear overhead. This happens during southern summer when the southern hemisphere is tilted towards the Sun.

TIME ZONES

The Earth is divided into 24 time zones. These run from north to south, a bit like lines of longitude. Time across the world is counted from the time at Greenwich, London, England. The time in places to the east of Greenwich is further ahead.

When it is 12 noon in Greenwich, it is 1 o'clock in the afternoon at places in the first time zone to the east, 2 o'clock at places in the second time zone and so on.

Moscow, in the USSR, is in the third time zone to the east. That means when it is 12 noon in England, it is 3 o'clock in the afternoon in Moscow.

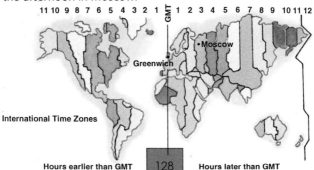

International Time Zones

Hours earlier than GMT   128   Hours later than GMT

New Zealand is twelve time zones ahead. This means that it would be midnight in New Zealand when it is noon in England.

New York is five time zones behind. This means that when it is noon in England it is 7 o'clock in the morning in New York.

DID YOU KNOW?

Some countries are so large that they have more than one time zone crossing them. Australia has three time zones, Africa has five and the United States of America has six!

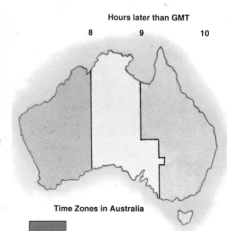

Hours later than GMT

8   9   10

Time Zones in Australia

THE ATMOSPHERE

THE AIR WE BREATHE

The Earth is surrounded by a mixture of gases we call the atmosphere. The atmosphere is split up into layers. Only the lowest layer has enough gas in it for us to breathe.

WHAT'S IN THE ATMOSPHERE?

The atmosphere is made up mainly of nitrogen (78%) and oxygen (21%). The other one percent is mainly argon. Lots of other gases are present in the atmosphere in tiny traces. These include carbon dioxide, neon, helium, krypton, hydrogen, xenon and ozone. Lots of dust particles are also in the atmosphere as well as a great deal of water vapour.

DID YOU KNOW?

There is so much water vapour in the atmosphere that if it all fell at once as rain, it would cover the Earth's land areas to a depth of 8 centimetres!

OXYGEN CYCLE

Oxygen is essential to humans and animals. Animals and humans all breathe in oxygen and give out carbon dioxide in turn. This carbon dioxide is taken in by plants which then give off oxygen!

LOWEST LAYER

The lowest layer of the atmosphere is the one we breathe. This is called the troposphere. The thickness of the troposphere varies. It is only 8km thick over the poles but is 18km over the equator. The troposphere is where the winds blow and where clouds form and rain falls.

TEMPERATURES IN THE ATMOSPHERE

LAYER	TEMPERATURE RANGE
Troposphere	15°C (sea level) -55°C (at a height of 18km)
Stratosphere	-55°C to 0°C
Mesosphere	0°C to -80°C
Thermosphere	-80°C to 2,200°C
Exosphere	2,200°C minimum

STRATOSPHERE

The next layer of the atmosphere is the stratosphere. This lies between 10km and 50km above the Earth's surface. The air in the stratosphere is too thin to breathe. Noctilucent clouds are found in the stratosphere. These clouds are thought to be made up of meteor dust.·

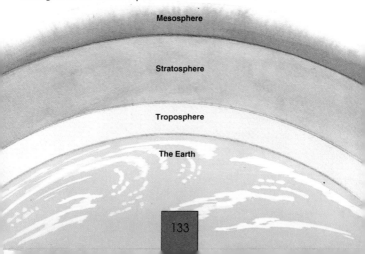

Mesosphere

Stratosphere

Troposphere

The Earth

PROTECTIVE OZONE

The ozone layer protects us from harmful rays from the Sun. Ozone is a type of oxygen gas. The bottom of the ozone layer lies about 25km above the Earth. Pollution has caused holes to appear in the ozone layer over the Arctic and Antarctic. Steps are now being taken to reduce this pollution and so protect the ozone layer.

DID YOU KNOW?

The ionosphere allows us to communicate by radio over long distances. This is because radio waves bounce back off the ionosphere. Radio waves travel at the speed of light. This is 300,000km every second. A radio wave can bounce off the ionosphere to the other side of the Earth in just a split second!

Ionosphere

THE UPPER ATMOSPHERE

Above the stratosphere is the mesosphere, which lies between 50km and 80km high. The ionosphere sits on top of the mesosphere. The ionosphere stretches from 80km high to around 500km. It gets its name from the fact that most of the air particles in it are ionized (electrically charged) by rays coming from space.

THE THINNEST LAYER

The exosphere is the thinnest and highest of the different layers of the atmosphere. It is made up mainly of hydrogen and helium, the lightest gases of all. The bottom of the exosphere is 500km above the Earth. From here, the atmosphere is extremely thin and stretches thousands of kilometres out into surrounding space.

Exosphere

The Earth

THE WEATHER

WEATHER WATCHERS

People have studied the weather for thousands of years. Many different ways of predicting the weather have been used. Centuries ago we used to depend on folklore to tell us what the weather would be like. We have all heard the old rhyme:

> Red sky at night, shepherd's delight
> Red sky at morning, shepherd's warning

This rhyme, as well as many of the others that were used, does have some truth behind it. There are different kinds of red sky some of which foretell rain and others which don't. It all really depends on the type of cloud that is seen at the time.

USING NATURE

Different plants can also be used to foretell the weather.
One good indicator is seaweed. If seaweed is damp and
slimy this is because there is moisture
in the air. This is a good sign that
rain is on the way. Some plants
close their petals when the
air is damp. Cones on larch
trees stay open during
fine weather but close
when rain is on the way.

MODERN METHODS

The old ways of foretelling the weather are interesting and
some are fairly reliable. However, it is better to rely on
modern methods for weather forecasting. Today we have
weather satellites orbiting the Earth. These are a tremendous
help when it comes to keeping a track on the movements of
clouds in the atmosphere.

WINDS

AIR PRESSURE

The Earth's atmosphere is pressing down on us. This is called atmospheric pressure, or air pressure. The higher you get above the ground, the lower the air pressure is.

CURRENTS OF AIR

The air rises over the equator where it is warmer. It then sinks over the poles where it is much colder. This means that huge currents of air are moving around the Earth. They rise high into the sky above the equator and move towards the poles. It then sinks as it gets colder. The air then moves across the Earth's surface from the poles and towards warmer areas.

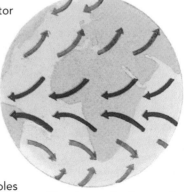

The red arrows show the warm air currents and the blue arrows show the cold air currents.

WHERE DO WINDS COME FROM?

Winds are caused by air moving from areas of high air pressure to areas of low air pressure. The pressure at the poles is greater than that at the equator. This is because air is sinking at the poles and rising at the equator. There is a worldwide system of winds. Trade winds blow near the equator. Westerlies blow midway between the poles and the equator. Polar winds blow at the poles.

GREAT WINDS

Huge whirling storms of wind and torrential rain form near the equator. Those that form in the Atlantic Ocean or Caribbean are called hurricanes. In the Indian Ocean they are called tropical cyclones and in the Pacific Ocean they are known as typhoons. The hurricane winds that hit England in 1987 and 1990 were the strongest winds there for 300 years!

WIND SCALE

In 1806 Francis Beaufort devised a system of recording wind speed. This is called the Beaufort Scale. It ranges from 0 to 12. Calm air is shown as 0 and hurricanes as 12.

THE BEAUFORT SCALE

SCALE	WIND SPEED (km per hour)	EFFECT OF WIND
0	0 - 1	CALM: Smoke goes straight up
1	1 - 5	LIGHT AIR: Smoke drifts slightly
2	6 - 11	LIGHT BREEZE: Wind felt on face; leaves rustle in trees
3	12 - 19	GENTLE BREEZE: Leaves and small twigs move all the time; small flags are blown out
4	20 - 28	MODERATE WIND: Small branches move in trees; dust and paper lifted

SCALE	WIND SPEED (km per hour)	EFFECT OF WIND
5	29 - 38	FRESH WIND: Small trees sway slightly; small waves formed on pools and lakes
6	39 - 49	STRONG WIND: Large branches move; wires whistle; umbrellas hard to use
7	50 - 61	NEAR GALE: Difficult to walk in wind; whole trees sway in wind
8	62 - 74	GALES: Walking very difficult; twigs are broken from trees
9	75 - 88	STRONG GALE: Slight damage to buildings
10	89 - 102	STORM: Trees can be uprooted; heavy damage to buildings
11	103 - 117	VIOLENT STORM: Widespread damage
12	118 or more	HURRICANE: Strongest winds of all

HIGHEST WIND SPEED

The highest ever recorded wind speed was on 12th April 1934 at Mount Washington, New Hampshire, United States of America where the wind was travelling at 371 kilometres per hour. This is more than three times as strong as hurricane force on the Beaufort Scale!

WINDIEST PLACE

The windiest place on Earth is Commonwealth Bay in Antarctica where gales reach over 300 kilometres per hour.

Antarctica

CLOUDS

AIRBORNE WATER VAPOUR

Clouds are formed from tiny droplets of water vapour or small ice crystals. These collect on microscopic dust particles. The particles float in huge masses in the atmosphere. We call these masses clouds.

TINY PARTICLES

The droplets which form clouds are so light that they float in the air. They measure about 0.02 millimetres across. They are so small that they could be placed on the point of a pin!

DID YOU KNOW?

About half the Earth is covered with cloud at any one time. These clouds can be seen from weather satellites high above the Earth's surface. Satellites help us to follow the movements of clouds with great accuracy.

CLOUD TYPES

There are only three main types of clouds. Cumulus clouds are fluffy shaped. Stratus clouds look like layers in the sky. Some clouds are thin and wispy and are seen high in the sky. These are the cirrus clouds.

Cumulus

Stratus

Nimbostratus

MIXTURES

Some clouds are a mixture of more than one of the main cloud types. For example, cirrostratus clouds are thin and milky-looking and occur high up in the atmosphere. Stratocumulus clouds are layers of fluffy clouds which are low in the sky.

HIGH CLOUDS

The highest type of ordinary cloud are the cirrus clouds, which can form eight kilometres or more above the Earth. The water inside these clouds is extremely cold with a temperature of about minus 30°C.

BRINGERS OF RAIN

Although clouds are formed from water vapour, not all clouds bring rain. If a cloud moves into warmer air it evaporates and disappears. Cumulus clouds are usually associated with sunny weather. Clouds which bring rain have names starting or ending in either 'nimbo' or 'nimbus'. Nimbostratus clouds are low, grey clouds which produce a steady rainfall. Cumulonimbus clouds are huge, tall clouds which bring heavy rain or even thunderstorms.

WHAT A CLOUD WEIGHS

Although clouds float in the air, the particles in them may contain many tonnes of water. The water droplets in even a small cloud may together weigh up to 1,000 tonnes!

LIGHTS IN THE SKY

BANDS OF LIGHT

A prism is a wedge-shaped piece of glass. In the 17th century the English scientist Isaac Newton discovered that if he passed a ray of sunlight through a prism the light is split up into different colours. The colours he saw were red, orange, yellow, green, blue, indigo and violet. Isaac Newton figured out that white light was actually made up of these colours. This band of colours is called a spectrum.

RAINBOWS

During a shower of rain the tiny drops of rain can act like little prisms. When sunlight passes through the raindrops it is split up just like it is when it passes through a prism. What we see when this happens is an arc in the sky. This arc is called a rainbow. The rainbow has the same colours as the spectrum. Red is on the outside of the rainbow and violet on the inside.

146

HALOES

Sometimes a ring of light
can be seen around the
Moon. This is called
a lunar halo. It is
caused by
moonlight
bouncing off water
droplets in the
atmosphere.
Haloes look a
bit like rainbows
although they are
complete circles of
light and not just arches.

SATELLITES

WHAT IS A SATELLITE?

A satellite is a small object moving round a bigger one. Some satellites are natural. The Moon is a natural satellite of the Earth. Some satellites are artificial. In other words, they are man-made space craft which have been put into orbit by rockets or the Space Shuttle.

WE'RE WATCHING YOU!

The first artificial satellite was launched in 1957. Since then, thousands of satellites have been put into orbit around the Earth. Many are there to make life easier for us. These include weather satellites and satellites with special equipment to help scientists to keep an eye on the Earth.

TELEVISION

Television programmes are sent up to satellites. These are then sent back to Earth. They can be picked up by anyone who has a satellite receiver. Television programmes can be sent all over the world in this way.

DID YOU KNOW?

Satellites orbiting Earth use energy from the Sun to produce their electricity. Special solar cells, which look like wings reaching out from the satellite, collect solar energy. This is then changed into electrical energy. Some pocket calculators and watches are powered the same way.

SATELLITE ORBITS

POLAR ORBITS

Satellites orbit the Earth in different ways. Some satellites go round the Earth above the north and south poles. This means that they can watch the whole Earth. This is made possible because the Earth is spinning below them. Each time the satellite passes over, a different part of our planet is underneath it. These orbits are called POLAR orbits.

GEO-STATIONARY ORBITS

The higher up a satellite is, the longer it takes to go round the Earth. Satellites whose orbits are 36,000 km above the Earth go round the Earth once every 24 hours. But, as we know, the Earth also spins on its axis once every 24 hours. So this means that the satellite 'keeps pace' with the part of the Earth directly below it. In other words, it stays in the same position above the Earth all the time. These orbits are called geo-stationary orbits.

WEATHER SATELLITES

KEEPING AN EYE ON THE WEATHER

Weather satellites travel around the Earth in geo-stationary orbits. This lets them keep an eye on the weather for the same area of the Earth's surface all the time. Different countries have their own weather satellites in orbit above their own countries which help meteorologists study the weather in these areas.

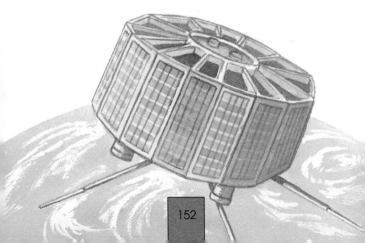

HOW WE GET THE INFORMATION

The data obtained by weather satellites is beamed down to special ground stations. It is then changed into images and information and sent back up to the weather satellite. The satellite then beams the information down to thousands of users across the globe.

DID YOU KNOW?

The European Space Agency operates the Meteosat weather satellites. These orbit the Earth high above the Atlantic Ocean. The images from Meteosat are an everyday feature of television screens all across Europe.

HOW WEATHER SATELLITES HELP US

AIR SAFETY
Before taking off,
aircraft flight routes
can be changed to
avoid any storms
and strong winds
that may put the
aircraft at risk.

SAVING LIVES
Many lives have been saved by weather satellites. If a
hurricane or severe storm is moving towards certain areas,
the people living there can be warned to get out of the way
before it reaches them.

ELECTRICITY
If cold weather is on the way electricity producers here on
Earth can produce more energy to meet the higher needs.

ROAD SAFETY

Road safety is also helped by weather satellites. If heavy snow is on the way, weather satellites can forecast this. This lets us get snow ploughs and road gritters ready in time to clear the roads.

WANT A SUN TAN?

Going to the seaside? Weather satellites can help you to choose a place that will be warm and sunny. Or they can tell us whether it is going to be rainy everywhere, so you can stay at home!

NOTHING NEW

The water that falls as rain has been around for millions of years. No new water is ever made. All the water that falls as rain has fallen as rain, snow or hail many times before. Water on the ground slowly becomes water vapour and goes up into the air. We call this evaporation. Water evaporates into the atmosphere from many different places, such as the seas and oceans, lakes and the leaves of plants. It eventually falls back to Earth as rain, snow or hail. It then goes back into the seas and oceans and lakes and is taken in again by plants. The water is continually reused. When the water is used again and again this way we call it the water cycle.

BLUE SKIES

The light from the Sun is actually
a mixture of other colours. Our
sky appears to be blue because
the blue light in sunlight is
scattered across the sky by the
gases in the atmosphere. The
atmospheres on other planets
are different to ours. The sky
from their surfaces may appear
a different colour altogether.

HAIL

Hailstones are formed when small droplets of frozen
rain form inside thunderclouds at heights of around
10 kilometres. The particles start to fall but are then taken
back up again by upward movements of air inside the cloud.
This happens a number of times. Each time it rises the
droplets get an extra coating of ice. Eventually, they
become heavy enough to fall all the way to the Earth.

SNOW

Snow forms as ice crystals on dust particles inside very cold clouds. When heavy enough they fall down through the clouds. Providing the temperature is low enough they remain frozen until they reach the ground. Snow doesn't normally fall as individual crystals. Usually a number of crystals gather together to form a snowflake. Large snowflakes can be as much as 5cm across. Each snowflake contains ice crystals of different shapes and sizes and it is said that no two snowflakes are ever exactly the same.

FROST AND DEW

If the night has been cold, you can often see a layer of moisture on the ground in the morning. This is called dew. This is because cold air can hold less water vapour than warm air. The water vapour in the cold air turns into water droplets and settles on the ground. If the temperature is below freezing point, the dew appears as a layer of frost.

HUMIDITY

Humidity is a measure of the amount of water vapour in the air. Warm air can hold more water vapour than cold air. Your skin can feel very sticky when the humidity is high. This is because the sweat given off by your skin to keep you cool can't evaporate away from your body.

FUTURE WEATHER FORECASTING

Satellites will play an even more important role in weather forecasting in the future. New satellites planned will be able to measure wind speeds, temperatures and humidity with great accuracy. This will allow us to predict the weather much more reliably.

WHAT ARE NATURAL RESOURCES?

There are two sorts of natural resources. The Earth provides lots of things that we use for power. These include wood from trees and water, coal, oil and gas from under the ground. Another kind of natural resource are things that are used to provide power. The flowing water in rivers and waves is used to generate electricity. Wind power is used in the same way. Solar panels are also used to collect sunlight to convert to electricity.

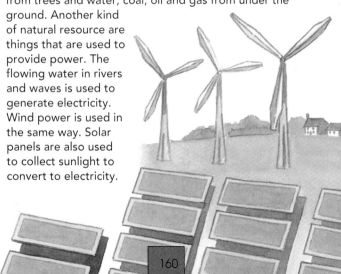

PREHISTORIC FUEL

Coal, oil and gas are known as fossil fuels. Fossils are the remains of animals and plants preserved in rocks. Fossil fuels were formed millions of years ago from the fossilized remains of plants. Coal, oil and gas have been around for a long time. However, we are using them up and they will run out eventually.

UNDER THE SEA

A lot of the oil we use comes from oil wells under the sea floor. This is obtained by oil rigs. There are two kinds of oil rig. The largest float on the sea and are anchored to the sea bed by huge cables. Fixed-leg rigs stand on legs that are attached to the sea bed.

DID YOU KNOW?

Some fixed-leg oil rigs are as tall as the Empire State Building in New York, USA, which is nearly 400 metres high!

OTHER PRODUCTS

We depend on coal and oil for many other things apart from
energy and lots of other products can be made from them.
These include perfumes, insecticides and antiseptics
which can be made from coal. Petrol, kerosene (jet fuel),
explosives, detergents, cosmetics and paint are all made
from oil.

RIVER POWER

Many countries depend on the flowing water in rivers and waterfalls to generate most of their electricity. The water is used to drive turbines which in turn spin electricity generators. Nearly all the electricity in Norway is made in this way, as well as nearly all that used in Brazil.

HOT WATER

In Iceland, hot water is obtained from under the ground which is used to provide heat for homes and factories. There is plenty of hot water available. The capital city, Reykjavik, uses hot water piped from underground at the rate of 15,000 litres every minute.

POLLUTION

WHAT IS POLLUTION?

Pollution is where the environment is harmed by products of human activity. There are lots of different kinds of pollution. Many lakes, rivers and seas are polluted when waste from chemical factories is washed into the water. The sea is a huge rubbish tip! Every year millions of tonnes of rubbish are dumped at sea, including glass, tins and even waste food.

OTHER POLLUTION

Waste material from houses is called sewage. There are sewage farms where sewage is treated with chemicals and made into fertilizer. However, lots of sewage is dumped into the sea. Many beaches are polluted because of sewage drifting back to shore and the sea at many resorts is dangerous to swim in because of the sewage polluting the water.

OILY WATERS

A lot of the pollution at sea is from oil. This comes from lots of different sources. Oil rigs spill oil into the sea and there is also some waste from oil refining factories on the coast. Some ships lose fuel which also pollutes the sea.

TANKERS

Many tankers have run aground or been damaged by storms and have then spilled their cargo of oil into the sea. This can really damage the environment. In 1989 the oil tanker Exxon Valdez ran aground in Prince William Sound, Alaska. Nearly 50 million litres of oil were spilled into the sea. Many birds, fish and animals were caught in the oil and died.

THE GREENHOUSE EFFECT

When fossil fuels are burned carbon dioxide is given off. There is already carbon dioxide in the air. It is one of the gasses which creates the greenhouse effect (where some of the Sun's heat is trapped in the atmosphere which then keeps our planet warm).

TOO MUCH

Too much carbon dioxide in the atmosphere is dangerous. The Earth may warm up too much and affect the climate. Some scientists think that if this happens the ice caps may start to melt. If this happened many of the low-lying coastal areas may be flooded. To help reduce the greenhouse effect we must use other ways of making energy and burn less fossil fuels.

BAN THE CAR!!

The number of cars, buses and other road vehicles has increased greatly over the past few years. The fumes given off by cars pollutes the air and makes it dangerous to breathe. Some cyclists even have to wear face masks to filter out the fumes when they are cycling along some city streets.

NATURAL POLLUTION

Not all pollution is man-made. Some pollution comes from natural disasters such as volcanic eruptions, when a layer of ash may be scattered across the surrounding countryside.

SAVE THE ENVIRONMENT!

The human race makes a lot of rubbish! Every week we throw away glass bottles, tins, paper, plastic and many, many other things. This has to be put somewhere and is often buried in huge tips. Some of the rubbish is burned. But it costs a lot of money to make NEW glass bottles, tins, paper and plastic. So, the message is - recycle your rubbish. Whenever you can, put your rubbish into recycling bins. This really helps to save the environment.

TURN OFF THAT LIGHT!

Electricity is made in power stations. Many power stations burn fossil fuels to help them make energy. This increases the amount of carbon dioxide in the atmosphere. You can help to keep the amount of carbon dioxide down. Turn off unwanted lights. Get your mum and dad to insulate hot water tanks and pipes. Have a shower instead of a bath (you use less hot water). Insulate your loft. Make windows and doors draughtproof. By doing these things you will save electricity (and make the electricity bill smaller!). But, more importantly, you will help the environment because the power stations will not need to make as much electricity, and so will burn less fossil fuels!

GLOSSARY

atmosphere
the mixture of gases which
surrounds the Earth

atoll
a circular coral island
surrounding a lagoon

Beaufort scale
the scale by which the speed
of winds are measured

calcite
the main part of limestone rocks
which is dissolved by the acid
that is formed as water seeps
through the rock

canyon
a deep, narrow valley

cloud
a mass of tiny droplets of
water vapour floating in the air

continent
one of the Earth's large
land masses

continental drift
the movement of the continents
over the Earth's surface

continental plate
a piece of the Earth's crust

current
a flow of water in a definite
direction

delta
an area of sandbanks formed
at the mouth of a river

desert
an area where there is very
little rainfall and vegetation

dew
a layer of moisture formed as water vapour condenses out of the air and settles on the ground

Earth
one of nine planets orbiting the Sun

Earth's core
the hot centre of the Earth

Earth's crust
the hard, rocky outer layer of the Earth

Earth's mantle
the hot liquid region inside the Earth which lies between the core and the crust

earthquake
movements in the Earth's crust caused when two plates rub against each other

equator
the imaginary line running around the Earth exactly midway between the poles and which divides the Earth into two halves, or hemispheres

erosion
the wearing away of the rocks and soil of the Earth's crust

estuary
a broad river mouth where tides occur

forest
a large area with a heavy growth of trees and plants

frost
frozen dew

greenhouse effect
the build up of certain gases
in the Earth's atmosphere
which traps the Sun's heat
and warms up the climate

hail
droplets of frozen rain formed
inside thunderclouds

halo
a ring of light around the
Moon caused by moonlight
reflecting off droplets of
water vapour in the atmosphere

hemisphere
one of two halves of the Earth

humidity
the amount of water vapour
in the air

hurricane
huge swirling storms of wind

and torrential rain which form
near the equator

island
an area of land surrounded
by water

lagoon
a circular-shaped area of shallow
salt water surrounded by an atoll

lake
an inland area of water which
is located in a low-lying area
of land

landslide
a downward movement of
soil and rocks

lava
molten rock which comes out
of volcanoes from beneath
the Earth's crust

mountain
a hill of great size

ocean
a large area of salt water

orbit
the path of a smaller object around a larger one, such as the Moon around the Earth or the Earth around the Sun

permafrost
deep layers of soil which remain frozen even during the summer months

poles
the cold regions at the very north and south of the Earth

pollution
where an area is harmed by products of human activity

such as an oil slick at sea or a cloud of poisonous gases in the atmosphere

pothole
a hole in the ground worn away by rainwater

rain
water falling in drops from the clouds

rainbow
a band of light seen in the sky formed from sunlight passing through raindrops

Richter scale
the scale by which the power of earthquakes are measured

river
water which flows across the land

satellite
A small object which orbits a larger one. The Moon is a satellite of the Earth. The Earth is a satellite of the Sun

sea
an area of salt water that is smaller than an ocean

snow
ice crystals formed on dust particles inside very cold clouds

solar system
the Sun and other objects, like planets, that travel around it

stalactite
an icicle-like object which forms on the roof of a cave and is made up of solidified calcite entering the cave through the roof

stalagmite
an icicle-like object built up from calcite which falls from the roof of a cave and solidifies on the cave floor

star
an object in space which shines by making its own light

sun
the star which lies at the centre of our Solar System and which gives the Earth and other planets their light and heat

supercontinent
a large land mass formed by two continents drifting together

tide
the rise and fall of sea level caused by the gravity of the Sun and Moon

trench
huge valleys on the ocean floor where one continental plate is dragged beneath another

tropical cyclone
a hurricane which forms in the Indian Ocean

tundra
areas of frozen treeless land found at high latitudes close to the Earth's north polar region

typhoon
a hurricane which forms in the Pacific Ocean

volcano
places where lava comes up through the Earth's crust

waterfall
a place on a river where the water flows over a steep drop

wave
a ridge on the surface of water caused by wind blowing across the surface

wind
the movement of air across the Earth's surface

year
the time it takes for the Earth (or any other planet) to travel once around the Sun

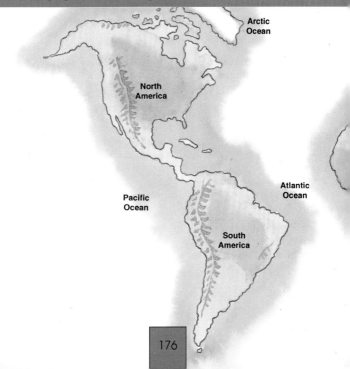

Arctic
Ocean

North
America

Atlantic
Ocean

Pacific
Ocean

South
America

176

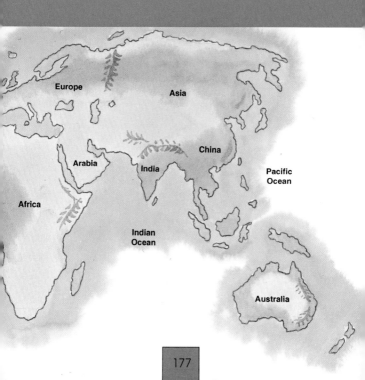

Europe

Asia

China

Arabia

India

Pacific
Ocean

Africa

Indian
Ocean

Australia

THE ARCTIC

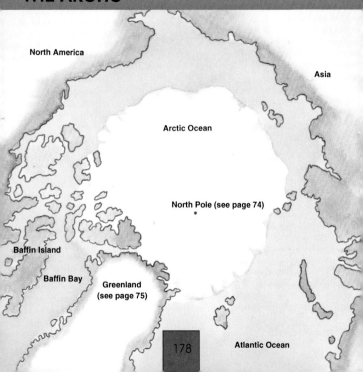

North America

Asia

Arctic Ocean

North Pole (see page 74)

Baffin Island

Baffin Bay

Greenland
(see page 75)

178

Atlantic Ocean

ANTARCTICA

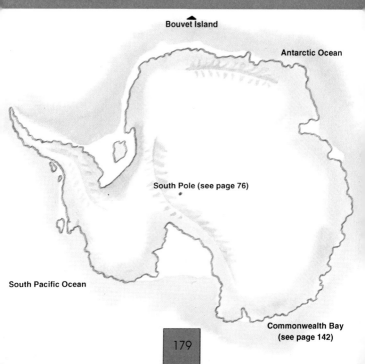

Bouvet Island

Antarctic Ocean

South Pole (see page 76)

South Pacific Ocean

Commonwealth Bay
(see page 142)

NORTH AMERICA & CANADA

Aleutian Islands

Alaska

Arctic Ocean

Greenland

Canada

Hudson Bay

Newfoundland

The Great Lakes

Mount Washington (see page 142)

Rocky Mountains

Niagara Falls (see page 96)

Bay of Fundy

United States

Death Valley

Grand Canyon (see page 93)

Atlantic Ocean

Carlsbad (see pages 69 & 71)

Pacific Ocean

Gulf of Mexico

Mexico

Caribbean Sea

South America

SOUTH AMERICA

◄ Hawaii

Atlantic Ocean

Venezuela

Colombia

Galapagos Islands ▼

Ecuador

R. Amazon (see page 94)

Andes Mountains
(see page 60)

Brazil

Peru

◄ Lake Titicaca (see page 91)

Bolivia

Pacific Ocean

Paraguay

Chile

Uruguay

Argentina

South Atlantic Ocean

Polar desert and tundra

Tropical rainforest

182

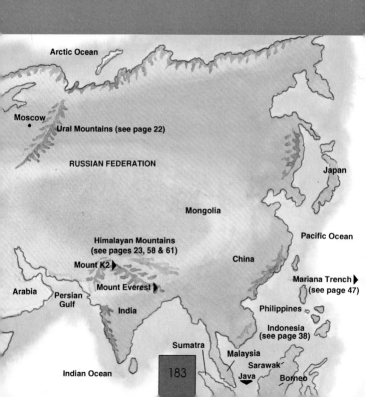

Arctic Ocean

Moscow

Ural Mountains (see page 22)

RUSSIAN FEDERATION

Japan

Mongolia

Pacific Ocean

Himalayan Mountains
(see pages 23, 58 & 61)

Mount K2 ▶

China

Mariana Trench ▶
(see page 47)

Mount Everest ▶

Arabia

Persian
Gulf

India

Philippines

Indonesia
(see page 38)

Sumatra

Malaysia

Indian Ocean

Sarawak

Java

Borneo

183

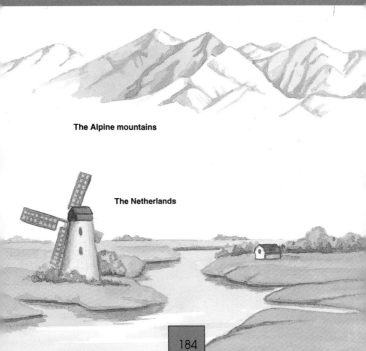

The Alpine mountains

The Netherlands

Iceland

Scandinavia

Baltic
Sea
(see page 42)

RUSSIAN FEDERATION

North Sea

Ireland

County Clare →
(see page 69)

United
Kingdom

London

Netherlands

Poland

Germany

Atlantic Ocean

France

The Alps

Romania

Bulgaria

Black Sea

Pyrenees Mountains
(see page 70)

Yugoslavia

Adriatic
Sea

Corsica

Italy

Spain

Sardinia

→ Sardinia

Greece

Turkey

Malaga (see page 68)

→ Sicily

Mediterranean Sea

AFRICA

Sahara Desert

Victoria Falls

Morocco

Mediterranean Sea

Israel

Dead Sea (see page 90)

Jordan

Algeria

Libya

Egypt

Arabia

Sahara Desert (see page 117)

Red Sea
(see page 42)

Mauritania

Mali

Niger

Chad

Sudan

Ethiopian
Highlands

Guinea

Uganda

Nigeria

Zaire

Ethiopia

Gulf of Guinea

Congo Basin

Kenya

The Great Rift Valley
(see page 23, 64 & 65)

Indian Ocean

Atlantic Ocean

Angola

Tanzania

Zambia

Mozambique

Namibia

Zimbabwe

Botswana

South Africa

AUSTRALASIA

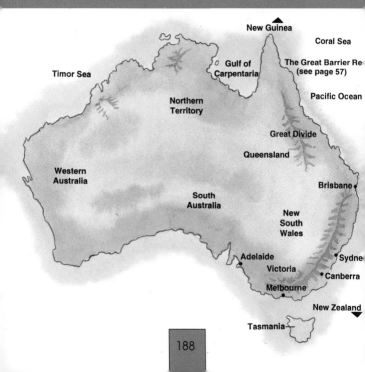

New Guinea

Coral Sea

Timor Sea

Gulf of
Carpentaria

The Great Barrier Re
(see page 57)

Pacific Ocean

Northern
Territory

Great Divide

Queensland

Western
Australia

Brisbane

South
Australia

New
South
Wales

Adelaide

Sydne

Victoria

Canberra

Melbourne

New Zealand

Tasmania

INDEX